Living
with
Potpourri

Written by
**Kate Lindley Jayne and
Claudette Suzanne Mautor**

Illustrated by
**Sandra Baenen and
Ellen Witteborg**

P

PETER PAUPER PRESS, INC.
WHITE PLAINS • NEW YORK

TABLE OF CONTENTS

INTRODUCTION

Potpourri captures the beauty and fragrance of a gardening year. Scents of flowers and leaves waft on gentle currents of air, bringing happy remembrances of many seasons. Color and scent of autumn are held after the last leaves have blown away. Living with potpourri is thoroughly enjoyable, and available to every person!

Dry herbs, garden and meadow wildflowers, and forest plants and trees may be used to advantage all year. Air-drying of plant material can be mastered in a short time; combining available material is as personal and varied as the family button box. Plants need not be destroyed to be used for potpourri. While a garden may be ruined by drought or flood, insects or critters, the potpourri enthusiast will treat each leaf and blossom with care for enjoyment and extended life.

Vegetable gardens, cutting and fragrant gardens, English or French gardens all serve a purpose and none is generally thought of as a potpourri garden. Yet, all can be the habitat of potpourri ingredients. Sassafras, witch-hazel, pine, honeysuckle, goldenrod, ironweed, and yarrow make substantial contribution to potpourri without inclusion in garden plans. So, if garden space is full, look beyond the garden fence, exchange with neighbors, gather from Mother Nature with courtesy.

Regardless of where one resides, flowers, shrubs and trees are available and adaptable. Herbs can be grown on windowsills, or be designed into a formal knot garden. Plants for potpourri are multitudinous and can satisfy most landscape designs, locations and personal preferences. To be introduced to plants by this minuscule glimpse into their world is a fascinating way to broaden knowledge and appreciation, and to be forever touched and gladdened by the bounties of nature.

HISTORY AND ORIGINS
OF POTPOURRI

No one knows when or why humans first
began using herbs, but it apparently was at
the dawn of history. Plants have been
appreciated ever since records were etched
or painted on cave or pyramid walls, but
while the plants were pictured, their uses
were unknown. Written history contains
volumes of nearly endless uses for plants, or
as the early writings say, "herbes."

Corn found at Bat Cave, New Mexico, dated
3,000 B.C. shows that Native Americans
cultivated and hybridized corn. Early writings
indicate that American Plains Indians used
many hundreds of herbs. Survival, while a
primary reason for herb gathering, was only
one purpose to which North American
Indians put natural plant materials. They also
used herbs for decoration, fragrance,
medicine, foods, and seasoning.

The Romans used herbs to honor heroes and
to put fragrance in houses. Many herbs held
in high esteem were given meanings
pertaining to health, prosperity and cleanliness. Beasts of burden benefited from the

Romans' knowledge of herbs; they used yellow loosestrife under the yokes of oxen to repel flies (this plant is still used today in repellent potpourris).

Basil, coming to us from the East Indies (and employed at present in cooking), was used in the 16th Century in "sweet bags." Consisting of basil and other fresh scented herbs, sweet bags were worn or carried as personal, individual potpourri. What a pleasing way to live with potpourri! A lullaby of the Maori of New Zealand tells of the neck locket or neck sachet. Dry herbs were used in some sachet types of potpourri while others consisted of the gummy resins left after processing the herbs.

Early European choices for scent included sweet marjoram, sweet basil, meadow sweet and orris. Later, lavender, rosemary, rose, violet, and scented geraniums were collected from the far-away tip of Africa, the Cape, and taken to Europe. There they were grown and loved in royal gardens.

Shortly after *Gerard's Herbal* (1597) recorded plants of the Middle Ages, European travelers abroad began to concentrate on collecting plants for their homelands. In 1640, John

Parkinson of Nottinghamshire, England, completed his *Theatrum Botanicum* in which he described 3,800 plants and their uses, and yet the treatise was not all-inclusive! English, French and Dutch explorers roamed the seas and oceans and returned with many plants new to their gardens. Monarchs of that time had apothecaries and gardeners go to foreign lands to sketch, paint, and collect plants. Iris, cultivated in European gardens since classical times, soon had the company of the Oriental poppy from Syria (1702), rhododendron from Turkey (1701), tulip, hyacinth, peony, and narcissus, along with an increasing number of others.

South Africa above the Cape provided the scented geranium (Pelargonium), heathers (Calluna), freesia, aloe, amaryllis, lobelia, and gladiolus.

Explorations continued and plants found their way from South America into European palace gardens, and eventually to the New World with early settlers. Zinnia was found in Mexico in 1796, and Fuchsia magellanica in 1823. Abutilon from the southern end of Chile made its European debut in 1837, as did Fuchsia fulgens, discovered the same year in Mexico.

In North America, exploration and plant gathering were pursued actively from the Mississippi River to the Pacific Ocean in the late 18th and through the 19th Centuries. California was covered with annuals, flowering shrubs, and giant trees. The plains area blossomed profusely for miles. The Rocky Mountains were magnificently clothed in forests of mammoth trees awaiting the adventurous botanist, missionary and explorer.

From Australia during this period came findings of unique plants. Many were indigenous to the continent; few had relatives elsewhere. Over 500 species of eucalyptus, for example, grew only in Australia proper and on its island state of Tasmania.

From Asia, hydrangea, rhododendron, begonia, buddleia, magnolia, clematis, astilbe, anemone, primula and a vast number of other plants were transported to Europe to fill conservatories, gardens and florist shops.

Traveling to little known parts of the world, in times past, was done at a reasonable pace by horse, mule, camel, sail, or foot, thus affording travelers ample time to write journals and to enjoy the marvels of nature revealed by the plants they had identified.

When these people, whether botanists, missionaries, or explorers, made campsites or entered villages and towns, they often stayed for a considerable time. From these base locations they would take day journeys to collect, then return and write. Their journals attest to their successes, and to their observation of the cultures they visited. In this way, they acquired knowledge of the uses of the plants, along with the correct combinations of plants for these uses.

Being hospitable is as old a custom as is the use of herbs. Strangers to foreign places watched and learned, asked and were shown, and hence wrote all they could about the many different customs related to plants, including their uses as seasoning for food. Tastes differ from country to country, yet all peoples season their cooking, as the travelers discovered.

Japanese gardening and the art of Bonsai were studied and copied world-wide.

American customs for using herbs and potpourri were a blend of several sources. Plants and customary herbal uses introduced to Europe made their way to America where they merged with North American Indian lore and practice. From the formal gardens of England and France to the wildflower fields in Colonial America, needs might remain unchanged while availability, variety, climate and physical circumstances could be vastly different.

All hands and energies were needed to survive in the New World. Rudimentary gardens provided food; beauty and fragrance were garden extravagances. Native flowers, along with a few marigold and marjoram seeds brought by ship, were used to brighten and freshen the houses and gardens of Colonial America. Since it was not practical to garden strictly for beauty and fragrance, gathering herbs and flowers was combined with the gathering of nuts and fruit to store for winter nourishment. Fragrant plants, roots and branches were collected with joy, and became an integral part of the American use of potpourri.

Today, every garden, meadow and roadside is a veritable storehouse of potpourri waiting to be rediscovered. The search for ingredients continues even in today's gardens, be they high-tech or primitive cottage, formal or casual, trimmed or untrimmed, annual or perennial, large or small, private or public, north or south, east or west, established or still in the planning. The manner in which herbs are used for potpourri continues to develop; each maker's discoveries are important.

Potpourri, though varied in content, has been used universally for centuries, and people have always had their favorite herbs and applications for them. The use of herbs is as much a part of the heritage of humans as is our use of fire, shelter, tools, and clothing, and it is just as fascinating to document.

Love of plants, it seems, transcends time and culture. What the Greeks and Romans found soothing, fragrant, and curative in plants has, by science, been reconfirmed in the present. Queens knighted mighty sailing heroes and commissioned great expeditions to seek herbs of foreign lands. Hospitable peoples shared their love of plants and plant lore with European strangers.

Scarcity haunts various resources of the globe. Plants of the world are prone to depletion; yet, unnamed varieties and species are being found still and millions of hybrid plants grace the planet. There are plants, such as poison ivy, to avoid, and endangered species to be left untouched. The useable plants compound their practicality with multiple purposes and significances.

Thus, when we spend happy winter hours poring over garden catalogues in rapt contemplation of spring and summer delights to come, we have at our fingertips the accumulated wisdom of the ages from peoples around the globe, brought to us by centuries of travelers and explorers. As we plant our herb gardens and prepare flavorful and multi-colored potpourri, we gratefully acknowledge those who have prepared the way.

COLOR, TEXTURE, FRAGRANCE, FLAVOR

Color, texture, fragrance and flavor are the keys to fine potpourri. The plants providing these keys are widely available in the wild or for purchase. The following list of annuals, perennials, trees, and shrubs emphasizes plants that are readily available and easy to grow.

COLOR:

Yellow/orange:

calendula
daffodil
goldenrod
pansy

strawflower
santolina
tansy

Pink/lavender:

allium
baby's breath
bee balm
geranium
globe amaranth
heather

heath
lavender
rose
strawflower
yarrow

Red/purple:

bee balm

salvia

| globe amaranth | strawflower |
| rose | xeranthemum |

Blue:

| bachelor button | mint |
| hyssop | salvia |

White:

| bee balm | strawflower |
| mint | yarrow |

TEXTURE:

artemisia	palm
baby's breath	pine cones
grasses	pods
ground pine	statice

FRAGRANCE:

anise hyssop	mints
artemisias	pine
bayberry	rosemary
cardamom	roses
geraniums, scented	salvia
hyssop	santolinas
lavender	tansy
lemon balm	thymes

FLAVOR:

allium
chamomile
geranium, scented
lavender
lemon balm
marjoram
mint
oregano

parsley
rosemary
sage
savory
sweet bay
tarragon
thyme

PLANTS FOR POTPOURRI

The garden contains plants with uses beyond
color, fragrance and texture. To employ the
plants for potpourri, it is important to
choose the correct part of each herb/plant.
Check recipes and other herb books for
specific plant parts to use if making
potpourri with plants other than those listed.
In general, flowers provide the color and
leaves the scent.

Name	Part Used
Acorus calamus	Leaves
Agastache Anise hyssop	Leaves, flowers
Artemisia annua	Leaves, flowers
Bay, Sweet	Leaves
Benzoin	Berries, twigs
Cardamom	Leaves, root
Chamomile	Leaves, flowers
Eucalyptus	Leaves
Lavender	Leaves, flowers
Lemon Verbena	Leaves
Mints	Leaves, stems, flowers
Orris	Root, cut or ground (may cause allergic reaction)

Patchouli	Leaves
Rose	Flowers, fruit
Rosemary	Leaves
Sage	Leaves
Santolina	Leaves, flowers
Sassafras	Bark, leaves, root
Southernwood (Artemisia)	Leaves
Sweet Woodruff	Leaves, flowers
Tansy	Leaves, flowers
Thyme	Leaves, stems, flowers
Vanilla Grass	Root, leaves
Vetiver	Root, leaves
Violet	Flowers

PLANT FRAGRANCE

Fragrance and flower color seem to be interrelated. Fragrant white flowers are most abundant. The less intense a color, generally , the more intense a fragrance. While hybridizing has changed this rule, and an exception to the rule can always be found (red rose, yellow tulip), still, the naturally-occurring flowers fit the rule. Altitude, too, affects fragrance, with the more intense being at lower altitudes. Another fragrance rule is that thick-petaled flowers, such as magnolia and hyacinth, tend to have an abundance of fragrance.

Some plants store fragrance in the roots, as with vanilla grass, while others, such as lemon grass, scented geraniums and sassafras, have fragrant leaves and stems. When fragrance is in the leaves and stems, it generally is stronger and lasts longer than when it is in the flower.

Many parts of the plants, sometimes all parts, are used in potpourri. The flowers, leaves, roots, needles, stems, fruits, and seeds of plants are represented in potpourri recipes in later chapters.

Plant oils and resins containing fragrances release them to humid air. On a steamy afternoon, moisture-laden air makes mosquitoes echo, outlines soften, and garden scents as thick as pudding. Every invisible, suspended speck of moisture mysteriously holds the fragrance released by a plant and dances without choreography across open spaces, often transporting those nearby to times past and bringing soothing fragrant delights. Air, water, sun and plant oils create an intangible potpourri that is fantastic when it occurs spontaneously out-of-doors. Whether it is ocean salt spray or the whisper of pines that are making their indelible impression, we will remember them when again we meet those scents. All this, and more, comes from potpourri, from combining dry plant materials or plant oils.

Fresh leaves, as well as dry ones, have the capacity to release fragrance to the air. Heat and humidity make the bathroom or hot-tub area prime locations for potted fragrant-leaved herbs, and for potpourri. Stove-top simmers mimic weather peculiarities, produced indoors at will.

Since the smell of freshly-mown hay travels

with the breeze, it is clear that some plants release their fragrances when cut or crushed. Putting potpourri in an open bowl or basket on a table or dresser, ready for a casual stir or pinch, brings forth the stored aroma on request. Anytime or all of the time, potpourri is as obliging to give pleasure as are the plants from which it comes.

SIGNIFICANCE OF COLOR

Colors make statements, as do fragrance, shape, and texture. Each season bears distinct colors. Color plays important roles in religious custom, national costume, school and team uniforms.

Color can agitate emotions or subdue strong feelings, can be cool or warm, soft or harsh. There are primary and secondary colors, each with its own hue and shade. There is no short explanation for the many effects of color. Suffice it for now that the significance acquired by certain colors has survived the passage of time, the translation of languages, the worship patterns of millions, and the fashion trends of modern civilization. While the mystery, fable and lore of plants are incredibly intriguing, color adds another dimension to the interest of potpourri. Putting together a mix whose colors have known meanings will heighten the delight of these treasures.

WHITE: Protection, peace, happiness

abutilon   lotus
astilbe   pansy

baby's breath	phlox
daisy	rose
feverfew	statice
iris	xeranthemum

GREEN: Prosperity, luck, beauty, youth

artemisias	ivy
eucalyptus	oak
fern	pine
grasses	sage
ground pine	

BROWN: The home

cones	oak
grasses	pine
nuts	pods

PINK: Love, fidelity, friendship

astilbe	rose
globe amaranth	statice
heather	strawflower

RED: Strength, courage

| celosia | salvia |
| rose | strawflower |

YELLOW: Wisdom

daffodil	statice
goldenrod	strawflower
pansy	yarrow
santolina	

PURPLE: Power

globe amaranth	statice
heather	violet
sage	xeranthemum

BLUE: Peace, sleep

bachelor's buttons	statice
delphinium	violet
sage	

ORANGE: Success

calendula	geum
daisy	strawflower

UTILITARIAN POTPOURRI

Living with potpourri need not be limited to pleasing aromas for the human race. Animals and insects share in the history of fragrances and their addition to a pleasant existence. People have favorite flowers and herbs, being drawn to them for no explicable reason other than for pleasure.

Animals, too, seek out certain plants for their pleasure (cats - catnip) or cure (dogs - grass). Those animals recognized as grazers seek plants for sustenance and avoid the many that are poisonous.

Hummingbirds in the authors' native western North Carolina return each year to rest in the giant goldenrod at the edge of a pinewoods. Insects enjoy favorite, tasty herbs, though at times to the consternation of humans! Then, again, notice that in contrast certain plants remain untouched by insect, beast, or man.

These observations are true, as surely as is "A Rose is a rose is a rose." So, let us use these facts as we describe the mixing of potpourri to deter the communing of insects with vertebrates and vegetation.

MOTH REPELLENT

2 cups Nicotiana or wild tobacco
⅛ cup rue
¼ cup wormwood
⅛ cup mugwort
½ cup santolina

Dried leaves and stems of the above ingredients, cut or broken, and blended make an effective repellent against moths. Place the mixture in cloth bags for use in closets, trunks, or dressers where woolens are stored, to dissuade wool-moths from dining on woven treasures.

The mix may be added to mulch and compost, or be sprinkled at the base of plants or under shrubs. Rain and moisture will release the repellent, protecting the area from moths spending part of their life cycles there.

FLEA REPELLENT

1 cup eucalyptus
1 cup pennyroyal

In cave dwellings, medieval cottages and

Victorian mansions, tradition approved scattering herbs on floors to repel insects, as well as to emit pleasant fragrances. Late 20th Century custom deems such treatment of floors and carpets unsavory and untidy.

A combination of dried pennyroyal and eucalyptus, crushed and put into 5″ x 5″ cloth bags, is a useful addition to a pet's bed area. A basket of the mixture, topped with dried flowers for beauty and interest, may be set near entryways to deter the pesky fleas. Containers of the mix can be used under beds, couches and chairs for deterrence and fragrance.

Pennyroyals are low growing herbs; eucalyptus is a tree. Both can be started each year from seed and grown attractively in yard or garden.

FLY REPELLENT

1 cup wormwood
1 cup tansy
½ cup sandalwood
½ cup smartweed

Use these herbs dry and mixed by placing

them in open bowls or baskets in each room. Open windows and entryways are good locations for containers of the fresh, tart fragrance.

Wormwood and tansy are hardy perennials that make tall background plants for the garden. The wormwood has lacy blue-grey foliage; tansy is interesting for its frilly green leaves and yellow button flowers. Smartweed is prolific if given half a chance and is worth a remote space.

Smartweed (Polygonum sp.) is reportedly a fly repellent of benefit to horses and cattle. Picked fresh and rubbed on the animal daily, it repels hovering insects.

Bouquets of wormwood, tansy and smartweed, 12″ in length, 12-15 stems total, can be tied at the base and hung upside-down in doorways, on porches, or in outdoor picnic areas to repel insects. Long-stemmed flowers may be included for color. After they have dried completely, they can be added to repellent potpourris.

GARDEN PEST REPELLENT

1 sage plant - Salvia officinalis, purple sage
1 hyssop plant
1 pyrethrum plant
Marigold as convenient or desired

A living potpourri for the garden, these plants, grown there, will be untroubled by pests, when other plants may be marred or destroyed by ravenous insects. Planted among other favorites, they add fragrance, color (lavender, blue, yellow to orange, and white), and protection.

Properties in the chemical make-up of these herbs, as with others mentioned previously, repel insects. Pinch or clip leaves and scatter them around the garden area. During fall or spring garden-cleanup, save dry leaves, flowers, clippings of these herbs and add them to mulch, compost, or mix into the topsoil.

Sage, hyssop, and pyrethrum are hardy perennials; marigold can be grown easily from seed each season.

POTPOURRI FOR
THE DWELLING

The pleasures of fragrance from the garden
are enhanced by the ease of growing the
plants. The glorious colors and fragrances of
spring, summer and fall can be enjoyed
indoors year-round when potpourri is
involved.

The following recipes are especially good to
use throughout the house because living
with potpourri may be one of the most
rewarding ways to use garden herbs and
flowers. Whether fragrance for the house is
the goal, or special scents for the bath and
bedroom please better, each recipe may be
adjusted to suit your unique needs.

GENERAL INDOOR FRAGRANCE

Scented-leaf Geranium Potpourri

½ cup lime geranium
½ cup ginger geranium
½ cup orange geranium
½ cup strawberry geranium
½ cup lemon verbena

Geraniums with scented leaves are vigorous growers and thrive with occasional pruning. Save the accumulated leaves to make potpourri. Dry the leaves, which takes a week or so, then store them in a securely capped tin or dark-glass container.

Lemon verbena leaves dry more rapidly than do the geranium leaves and have an intense lemon smell which remains strong when exposed to air. The geraniums and verbena cannot survive frost but do flourish as long-lived houseplants.

Rose-Scented Potpourri

½ cup rose buds or rose petals
1½ cups old-fashioned rose geranium
1½ cups true rose geranium
½ teaspoon ground cloves

Home-grown roses and most wild roses have plentiful fragrance while many florist roses lack the beloved rose scent. If gathering rosebuds, pick them after dew or rain has evaporated. Pick the petals of open flowers before they fade and when dry, also.

Rose buds, because of their thickness, need

to dry thoroughly, and be stored separately from petals.

The clove spice is optional; it adds an indescribable depth to the rose scent as well as increases the longevity of the fragrance.

BATH

½ cup chamomile
½ cup lavender
1 cup mint
½ cup rosemary

The soothing soak of a hot bath can be like a dip in a natural hot spring, with the addition of an herbal potpourri. Gentle and alluring, this bouquet pleases the senses.

Combine the dry ingredients. Put ¼ cup of the mix into a muslin bag to hang under the water tap as the tub fills. For a steamy, fragrant shower, hang a bag of potpourri at the showerhead. Gently rub the bag of fragrance on the skin for a final burst of scent.

BEDROOM

½ cup Artemisia annua
1 cup cardamom
½ cup mint
½ cup rose petals
¼ cup sage

This recipe offers a variety of scents.
Differing degrees of humidity, and an
occasional stir or pinch, bring delicate
variations of the fragrance to notice.

Cardamom is a tropical plant, and should be
grown in the house or conservatory. The
leaves are tall and require cutting, when dry,
into one-inch or smaller pieces. Artemisia
annua grows well outdoors and will self-seed.
Variegated pineapple mint, orange mint and
lemon bergamot mint are especially good in
this recipe.

LINENS

Just as it seems that potpourri recipes have
filled our senses, rid our rooms and gardens
of pests and satisfied our hard-to-buy-for gift
list, here come more interesting ways to

employ herbs and spices. To freshen and protect linens, make a batch of potpourri from the following recipe:

½ cup anise hyssop
1 cup sweet bay
1 cup eucalyptus
½ cup lemon verbena
¼ cup santolina
¼ cup Artemisia southernwood

To keep the freshness of a clear summer day in linens, use this herbal potpourri in the closet. Put the dry herb mixture into a cloth bag or a box with small perforations in the sides. Place either one between the linens or on the shelf beside them.

These herbs provide a gentle and welcoming scent. Each one is known to have properties that repel insects, making this a fine potpourri to use when packing away off-season clothing. Tucking a bag of the mix into pockets of suitcases and handbags, or near shoe racks and in closet corners, is another way to enjoy the pleasure of some herbal company.

CELEBRATION AND HOLIDAY POTPOURRI

One of the most popular, endearing and traditional uses of potpourri is for special occasions. These memorable times of gathering people to reflect, share, and rejoice are enriched with visual, scent-filled and tasty treats. By using home-made potpourri for these occasions, one creates personal treasures and traditions. The symbolism of the plants and colors used strengthens the messages of love and family ties. The following recipes comprise a general guide for holiday potpourri.

ST. VALENTINE'S DAY

1 cup rose petals
1 cup rose hips
½ cup rosemary leaves
½ cup red dianthus blossoms
½ cup bachelor's button blossoms and
    leaves
1 cup honeysuckle flowers
½ cup mint leaves (apple mint best)

These herbs and flowers, dried in the summer and autumn, and stored in a closed,

dark container, give a whiff of early spring
and some lovable whimsy to Valentine's Day.
(See flower symbolism.) Fragrance evokes
what words may fail to express. Give a tin of
potpourri filled with your heart's wishes to a
friend or loved one. The day will linger, the
feelings will have substance.

CHRISTMAS

Christmas is a time to be at home, or
dreaming of past holidays, a time to be
comfortable and mellow. Holiday traditions
are founded in love, worship, sharing, giving,
renewal and hope. The physical symbols
seem ageless, yet many, such as trees and
wreaths, favorite recipes and songs, change
with style and custom. To duplicate each
year the decorations of our childhood is
outside the realm of possibility for most. By
adding personal touches, a new tradition is
formed; with time it takes hold and becomes
another part of custom.

The remembrance of crisp winter smells is a
great part of the hustle and bustle, the
buying and wrapping, the cooking and
visiting at holiday time. Aromas no one can
forget come from cooking maple syrup,

popping corn for the tree, rolling rum balls, and baking gingerbread cookies. The scents of crackling fires, cool ocean breezes, pine needle garlands, or spicy orange pomanders are a potpourri of Christmas.

A more tangible mixture may be collected for special occasions:

1 quart fragrant pine needles
1 dozen small pine cones
1 cup bay leaves
1 cup bayberry leaves
3 cups sassafras leaves
3 cups orange peel
1 cup cinnamon sticks
½ cup whole cloves

Make this recipe by the (dry) gallon, as its popularity causes its disappearance by the basketful. A lot of pleasure comes with the gathering of needles and cones. Brown needles or fresh green ones can be used. If the needles are very long, they can be cut, by the handful, to about two inches in length. Cones, if larger than a teacup, may be incorporated after other ingredients are mixed. Bay leaves and bayberry leaves can be

left whole. Use oak, magnolia, orange or holly in place of, or in addition to the sassafras leaves. Tree leaves are used fresh or dry, with about one half of them crushed or broken at time of mixing. Save and dry orange and other citrus peels throughout the year for the potpourri. Cinnamon sticks broken to three-inch lengths or less, and whole cloves complete the recipe. Happy aromatic holidays!

THANKSGIVING

Here is a recipe with a twist—one for the birds. Looking skyward in the autumn, one frequently sees flocks of birds, some migrating, some in the area for the year. With a bit of food going their way, they will be a cheerful sight throughout the winter and into spring.

1 cup sage leaves
1 cup lovage leaves
½ cup pumpkin seed
½ cup squash seed
1 cup Indian corn
2 cups goldenrod
½ cup sunflower seed

1 cup evening primrose pods
2 cups basil leaves and flowers
2 cups hickory nuts
2 cups acorns

This large quantity makes a colorful, crisp, and fresh-scented mixture which is decorative in open glass containers for the holidays. After the festivities, it can be stored for later use as winter bird feed. The leaves will blow away, and the remaining nuts and seeds are attractive to foraging birds.

FLOWER AND HERB SYMBOLISM

Special occasions, such as weddings, anniversaries, and births, call for symbolic potpourri ingredients. One feels a strong attraction to certain plants, perhaps because of something felt, in addition to beauty and fragrance. Renaissance painters showed the strong emotions of love and hate via bouquets of flowers. Herbs and their symbolic meanings have become one with the giving of flowers. Maybe the following recipes will delight the grower, maker, or receiver with another view into the realm of plants.

WEDDING POTPOURRI

Plant	Symbolic Meaning
½ cup daisy, white	Innocence
1 cup daffodil	Regard
½ cup dogwood	Durability
¼ cup goat's rue	Reason
1 cup grasses	Utility
1 cup holly	Foresight
1 cup ivy	Friendship, fidelity
2 cups mint	Virtue
½ cup straw, whole	Union
1 cup sweet pea	Delicate pleasures

BIRTH POTPOURRI

Plant	Symbolic Meaning
1 cup bachelor's buttons	Single blessedness
½ cup dandelion	Oracle
1 cup hyssop	Cleanliness
1 cup mallow	Mildness
½ cup thyme	Activity, courage, strength
¼ cup valerian	An accommodating disposition
½ cup yellow violet	Rural happiness, loyalty, devotion

ANNIVERSARY POTPOURRI

Plant	Symbolic Meaning
½ cup campanula	Gratitude
1 cup daffodil	Regard
½ cup dogwood	Durability
1 cup oakleaf geranium	True friendship
1 cup rosemary	Remembrance
½ cup sorrel	Affection
½ cup white clover	Think of me
1 cup zinnia	Thoughts of absent friends

LOVE POTPOURRI

Plant	Symbolic Meaning
1 cup heliotrope	Devotion
1 cup myrtle	Love
½ cup pansy	Thoughts
½ cup peach blossom	I am your captive
½ cup red clover	Industry
1 cup rudbeckia	Justice
1 cup sage	Wisdom, virtue
½ cup xeranthemum	Cheerfulness under adversity

PLANTS AND THEIR SYMBOLIC MEANINGS

For easy reference, use this list of plants and their symbolic meanings to assemble potpourris to deliver unspoken messages.

Aloe . . . Healing, protection, affection
Angelica . . . Inspiration
Arbor vitae . . . Unchanging friendship
Bachelor's Buttons . . . Single blessedness
Basil . . . Good wishes, love
Bay . . . Glory
Carnation . . . Alas for my poor heart
Chamomile . . . Patience
Clover, white . . . Think of me
Fern . . . Sincerity
Geranium, oak leaved . . . True friendship
Goldenrod . . . Encouragement
Heliotrope . . . Eternal love
Holly . . . Hope
Hollyhock . . . Ambition
Honeysuckle . . . Bonds of love
Horehound . . . Health
Hyssop . . . Sacrifice, cleanliness
Ivy . . . Friendship, continuity
Lavender . . . Devotion, virtue
Lady's Mantle . . . Comforting
Marjoram . . . Joy, happiness

Mints . . . Eternal refreshment
Morning Glory . . . Affectation
Nasturtium . . . Patriotism
Oak . . . Strength
Pansy . . . Thoughts
Pine . . . Humility
Poppy, red . . . Consolation
Rose . . . Love
Rosemary . . . Remembrance
Rudbeckia . . . Justice
Rue . . . Grace, clear vision
Sage . . . Wisdom, immortality
Salvia, blue . . . I think of you
Salvia, red . . . Forever mine
Savory . . . Spice, interest
Southernwood . . . Constancy, jest
Sweet pea . . . Pleasures
Sweet woodruff . . . Humility
Tarragon . . . Lasting interest
Thyme . . . Courage, strength
Valerian . . . Readiness
Violet . . . Loyalty, devotion
Violet, blue . . . Faithfulness
Violet, yellow . . . Rural happiness
Willow . . . Sadness
Zinnia . . . Thoughts of absent friends

CULINARY/GOURMET POTPOURRI

While many grand and nourishing foods are delectable by themselves, the creative use of herbs adds variety to the food and enjoyment to the process.

The ingredients of favorite recipes can be mixed and stored in dark-glass or pottery jars for decoration as well as convenience. Favorite culinary herbs may be hung whole, or be arranged into a wreath or bouquet, adding another decorative element to the kitchen-dining area.

If the taste of lemon is a family favorite, then a potpourri of lemon balm, lemon verbena, and lemon-scented geranium leaves, dried, may be mixed for future use. A pinch for tea, a tablespoon for stove-top simmer, a muslin bagful for a fragrant bath, are only a thought and a twist of the lid away.

For a refreshing flavor change add a pinch of mint, licorice, lemon balm or rose geranium to recipes for pound, loaf or ring cakes.

The following recipes are offered as guides, not rules, to the use of herbs in simple and tasty cooking.

ROSE GERANIUM/LEMON VERBENA JELLIES

Make standard apple jelly, using several red-skinned apples or a handful of cranberries to add color to the juice. Pour the boiling jelly juice into pre-heated glasses containing either a rose geranium leaf or a lemon verbena leaf and seal as usual.

These jellies are divine on hot, fresh-baked breads or biscuits. For a refreshing respite from a busy day, sit beneath a fragrant lilac with a cup of hot tea and a plate of biscuits and herbed jellies. Either jelly, in place of mint sauce, is delicious with roast lamb.

TEA

Take from the garden herbs that please
Often a few make wonderful teas.
Take from the garden herbs to press
Often a few put an end to stress.
Take from the garden into the house
Herbs to be lived with by pound or by ounce.
                                        C. S. Mautor

Hang clean fresh-picked herbs in small bundles of 5-10 stems, until dry. Crush and store in closed tin or dark container. Hot or chilled tea made from one or a combination of the following ingredients should be measured for individual taste. Generally, one teaspoon of dry leaves makes one cup of tea. Some herbs will be stronger than others, requiring tempered measurement, again, by taste.

Calming & soothing tea:

feverfew	thyme
rosemary	sweet woodruff
sage	

Brisk, refreshing tea:

lemon balm
lemon verbena
mints - apple, ginger, spear, pepper

SOUP

— the secret is in the simmering —

¼ teaspoon savory
¼ teaspoon thyme (French, English, oregano)

½ teaspoon basil (sweet, dark opal)
¼ teaspoon oregano (Greek) (from dry herbs)

Add herbs for last ½ hour of simmering.
Recipe sufficient to flavor 6 cups soup. To
make a large quantity of the mixture, use
volumes in proportion to the above recipe,
and the soup potpourri will be ready when
you need it. For freshly harvested herbs, use
about twice these amounts. It's lovely to have
little bits of herbs in the soup, but if you
wish, you may put the herbs into a cheese
cloth.

STEW

6 cups stock
3 large potatoes
2 medium carrots
1 onion
2 pieces celery (1 cup)
Jerusalem artichokes (1 cup).
2 cups floured and browned diced meat
2 bay leaves
3 tablespoons chives
1½ tablespoons rocambole garlic
6 leaves basil fresh, or ½ teaspoon dry
½ teaspoon oregano thyme (dry measure)
½ teaspoon rosemary leaves (dry measure)

Cut vegetables into serving-sized pieces.
Cook in 6 cups stock with diced meat and
bay leaves. Chop fine or crush spices and add
to mixture for final half-hour of simmering.
Remove bay leaves and serve.

SALAD

1 bowl torn lettuce
10 leaves Good King Henry
12 leaves French sorrel
1 burnet leaf
1 lovage leaf
2-inch sprig fennel
3 tablespoons sweet marjoram
2 tablespoons French tarragon
2 tablespoons chives
3 tablespoons vinegar
2 tablespoons olive oil
12 calendula blossoms

Mince Good King Henry, sorrel, burnet, and
lovage, and add to bowl of torn lettuce.
Mince fennel, marjoram, tarragon, and chives,
and add. Mix vinegar and olive oil (you may
wish to use a ratio which favors the olive
oil), pour over greens, and toss salad. Place
12 or so fresh calendula blossoms on top.
Chill before serving.

VINEGARS

Dill, burnet, French tarragon, garlic, parsley, chives, rosemary, French sorrel, sage, marjoram, and thyme, alone or in combination, make wonderful additions to vinegars. Use a cup of fresh, young leaves and stems, cut and/or bruised, per pint of white wine or cider vinegar. In a non-metal container, cover the herbs with vinegar and store for about 2 weeks. Shake jar occasionally. Repeat application of new herbs for additional strength. Filter vinegar, put a whole leaf in bottle for decoration, cap tightly and store.

STOVE TOP SIMMER

A tablespoon each of scented geranium, mint and lemon balm leaves simmered in 2 cups of water imparts a delightful fresh fragrance to any room. The lemon balm is especially good while cooking seafood. A spicy wintertime combination is ½ teaspoon cinnamon, 6 whole cloves, and ⅛ teaspoon nutmeg simmered in 2 cups water. This fragrance recalls scenes of pumpkin pie, celebrations and family gatherings.

A FINAL THOUGHT

A conclusion is possible for this book, but
ending does not apply to natural things. Each
flower, fragrance, color, meaning or use for
plants in Living with Potpourri has been
described briefly in these pages. An ending,
except unhappily by extinction, is unfathom-
able. So, slight in knowledge, and stricken
with admiration, awe, and inspiration by
nature's gifts, we hope for an eternity of skies
outlined by those majestic beings of the plant
world, the trees.

May every morning share the grace of
winged creatures and the indescribable
beauty and fragrance of herbs. And to all,
forever, may the secrets within each petal
and leaf continue to blossom and unfold.

COMMON/BOTANIC NAME CROSS-REFERENCE AND INDEX

Additional information about the plants mentioned in this book may be found in the gardening section of any library. The following list includes the botanic and the common names used herein. Common names are followed by botanic nomenclature. Example: Onion - Allium. Sp. refers to a single species; spp. to plural species. Page numbers where each plant appears are also included.

BIBLIOGRAPHY

Cunningham, Scott, *Encyclopedia of Magical Herbs* (Llewellyn Publications, 1985)

L H Bailey Hortorium, *Hortus III* (Macmillan, 1976)

Jayne, Kate and Fairman, *The Sandy Mush Herb Nursery Handbook Edition 6* (1987)

Johnson, Hugh, *Principles of Gardening* (Simon & Schuster, 1979)

Meyer, Clarence, *50 Years of the Herbalist Almanac* (Meyerbooks, 1977)

Pickston, Margaret, *The Language of Flowers* (Michael Joseph Ltd., 1968)

Terrell, John Upton and Donna M., *Indian Women of the Western Morning—Their Life in Early America* (Anchor/Doubleday, 1976)

Wilder, Louise Beebe, *The Fragrant Garden* (Dover, 1974)

Copyright © 1988
Peter Pauper Press, Inc.
202 Mamaroneck Avenue
White Plains, NY 10601
ISBN 0-88088-401-0
Library of Congress No. 88-60659
Printed in Hong Kong
5   4   3   2